THE
Front Garden

HALF TITLE
Erlestoke, Wiltshire

TITLE PAGE
Kellaways, Wiltshire.
A cottage garden untouched by time, probably much as it
was when the cottage was built in the eighteenth century.

THE
Front Garden

Candida Lycett Green + Christopher Sykes

ELM TREE BOOKS · London

For my father, J.B.

First published in Great Britain 1981
by Elm Tree Books/Hamish Hamilton Ltd
Garden House 57–59 Long Acre London WC2E 9JZ

Copyright © 1981 Candida Lycett Green and
Christopher Sykes

Book design by Norman Reynolds

British Library Cataloguing in Publication Data

Lycett Green, Candida
  The front garden.
  1. Front gardens—England
  I. Title
  712'.6'0942   SB453.3.G7
  ISBN 0-241-10548-X

Photoset in Great Britain by Photobooks (Bristol) Ltd
Printed in Hong Kong by Wing King Tong Co Ltd

Contents

Introduction

ENGLAND is thick with wonderful front gardens—there is nowhere in the world that can boast any half as good. My definition of a front garden is one that can be seen in its entirety from the road or pavement and is thus open to public gaze—a different thing altogether from the back garden which is a much more private affair. Front gardens are invariably created to give as much pleasure to the passer-by as they do to their owners and it was for this reason that I wanted to put them into a book. They are crying out to be noticed and yet so often they are overlooked or taken for granted. It's the great grand gardens like Stourhead and Blenheim which have all the books written about them and all the acclaim, while myriad small masterpieces go quietly unrecorded. This book is meant to put the record straight—it's a celebration of front gardens and hopefully a source of inspiration and new ideas.

I have tried to illustrate as wide a cross section of front gardens as possible and inevitably they have fallen into two categories: formal and informal. At the most informal end of the scale are the vegetable front gardens which probably resemble most the original cottage gardens of England. These were first and foremost a source of food, until monastery gardens and hedgerows inspired the introduction of flowers wherever the vegetables and one or two fruit trees allowed a space. Gradually, as the necessity for self-sufficiency dwindled, the vegetables became less important and the flowers more abundant until the traditional cottage garden evolved, and subsequently the informal variations thereon. Of course that sweet disorder of hollyhocks, honeysuckle and lavender cannot happen in an instant and, although one or two of the cottage gardens in this book go back a hundred years to their owners' certain knowledge, and probably much more than that, I think you need a minimum of four years to create an established-looking and seemingly uncontrived effect. On the other hand the formal garden can be created far more quickly, and seems to be much the most popular form of gardening today. Bulbs planted in the autumn for a wealth of spring bloom mixed with wallflowers and forget-me-nots are then replaced by bedding-out annuals which spread their colour over the summer months, reaching their peak in August and early September. Bedding-out patterns and colour combinations of lobelia, tagetes, petunias and salvias etc, can be varied infinitely each year. For the tidy-minded it is an extremely satisfactory way of gardening.

Of course not every front plot divides exactly between these neater or wilder shores of gardening; there are often combinations of the two, and also the more unusual categories of front gar-gens, such as topiaries. These sculptures in yew, box or privet range from the traditional single bird or architectural shape (originally copied from grand Elizabethan gardens at the big house up the road), to extravagantly imaginative replicas of horses and battleships. Then there are the ornamental gardens where fantasy worlds are created with the help of rocks, shells, cement, papier mâché, broken china, cartwheels and of course gnomes and other folk who can now be bought at most garden centres. And then, finally, there are banks and verges, which in a way are the most astounding front gardens of all, simply because some of their owners cannot see them at all from their own houses and admit they are created to brighten up the street —for other people to enjoy.

I love every single garden in this book—they are all gardens which stopped me in my tracks and made me want to stand and stare, and they are all works of art in their own way. Each one is a little country of its own, and if you walk about in some of them you see different aspects carefully created by the owner to turn his garden into a miniature park, or a lush forest, or a portrait of his career—like the retired lock-keeper's house at Middlewich. What emerged from meeting and talking to the owners of these gardens was always the same. They were extremely contented people, more often that not in their sixties, seventies and sometimes eighties, and to say that the best gardens were created through love and happiness might sound corny, but it was my indisputable conclusion. Jack Saunders, who has a garden at Sherbourne near Burford, puts it far better than I:

There's something beautiful about producing something or assisting nature; actually you don't produce it, you assist nature, don't you? I had one chap along here and he said: 'You've got a lovely garden.' He said: 'Do you do it all yourself?' I said: 'Yes, with God's Help.' 'Ah,' he said, 'you leave it a twelvemonth and see what it's like. It'll be full of weeds.' And it would be, wouldn't it? That brings you back to religion: Man shall work with the sweat of his brow and eat the labours of his own hands, and that's it, isn't it? And that's what we've got to come back to and you'll come back to your ponies and traps and carts in time. I shan't be here, but somebody will be. I'd like to live it and do it all over again and live in the same place and have the same woman. There you are. And I hope I will end my song with her. I'm satisfied with her, I'm satisfied with my lot and I hope you people will be satisfied with the end of yours as I shall be when mine comes.

Perhaps that contentment and total lack of boredom has something to do with living in a state of constant anticipation—there is always something to look forward to in a garden. Perhaps, also, it is only retired people who can find the time needed for all that goes into a spectacular display—certainly there were few young people who owned the outstanding gardens. But I have a feeling that it's not just the time needed, it's a certain sort of pride which is fast being concreted over and replaced with a different sort—the pride of the motor car. The way we live now encourages drive-ins where flowers once flourished and the washing and polishing of cars rather than the pruning and mulching of roses. Nevertheless there is still a wealth of spectacular front gardens up and down the land and the variety and ingenuity of their creators is boundless.

The gardens are captioned as being in the counties to which they truly belong.

C.L.G.

ACKNOWLEDGMENTS

I would like to thank Margaret Adey, Ann Barnett, Jill Marshall and Sita Williams for finding some of these gardens, also Michael Russell, Rick Stroud, Eddie Mirzoeff, Ted Roberts, Andrew Parker Bowles, Martin Wilkinson, Caroline Somerset, David Mlinaric and Sarah Bulwer Long for lots of reasons, and my family for everything.

C.L.G.

Formal
Gardens

Chippenham, Wiltshire.
A spring display of polyanthus, daffodils, and tulips in beds shaped to
complement the architecture of the house.

MRS Frear's one extravagance is spring bulbs. She used to say to her husband, 'If I go before you, just smother me in spring flowers.' She spends £10 a year on bulbs. 'I just love them, and they give joy to a lot of people walking by—so cheerful to come home to—all just bursting.' Ever since 1938 when she and her late jusband first moved to the house, she has put on a fine display in the front. 'The first year of all I had 'Keizerskroon' tulips with heads as big as tea-pots. In the beginning the place was just bricks and rubble. Now people say, "You've got the best garden of the lot."' Mrs Frear digs up her bulbs when they're over and either plants them at the end of the back garden or gives them away. She then beds out snapdragons, stocks, marigolds, nemesias, dwarf dahlias and begonias. She visits many stately home gardens every year and her favourite, not unnaturally, is the valley of daffodils at Waddesdon. She puts soot and sheeps' droppings in the water butt which is her patent brew for producing healthy plants. 'Gardening is so much a question of intelligence,' says Mrs Frear. 'If you fill the garden full to choke with flowers, you don't get any weeds.' (Perhaps that is why her neighbours never seem to see her working out there.) 'Anyway, if you don't have enough colour the whole thing is something of nothing.' Her favourite flowers are the ones that come first, snowdrops and crocuses, 'though you must admit', she says, 'you won't find much to beat my daffs ('King Alfred') and tulips (mixed 'Darwin') this year.'

Kington Langley, Wiltshire. Mr Benham's, Mr Riley's and Mr Richardson's side-by-side gardens have become a famous local attraction.

LEFT
Malton, Yorkshire. The forget-me-not was supposed to ensure that those wearing it should never be forgotten by their lovers, however it has another, less pleasant, name—scorpion grass.

ABOVE
Charlbury, Oxfordshire. Mr Hughes lays out a different colour scheme every year and usually wins the best kept garden competition.

LEFT
West Lynn, Norfolk. An uncommon mixture of bedding plants and perennials including double daisies, wallflowers, mimulus, polyanthus and peonies.

RIGHT
Frome, Somerset. 'Showgirl' geraniums predominate in the hanging basket. 'Mrs Popple' fuchsias and mixed petunias in the foreground.

WHEN they had dairy cattle on their farm the Grays couldn't have much of a front garden because the cows used to eat everything. Although they've lived here thirty years this is only the fourth summer of the new front garden and the fourth summer without dairy cattle. Mrs Gray is the gardener of the family. 'It's really my main interest,' she says, 'and I do love it when passers-by stop to look.' Mrs Gray was brought up near Stourbridge on an isolated farm and she remembers there being masses of delphiniums in the garden. She still has some in her own garden but roses and chrysanthemums are her favourites. The house faces north and Mrs Gray says she would never have chosen red flowers if it had faced south. As it is, the red of the 'Topsi' roses and multiflora begonias become almost fluorescent in the twilight. 'It's a real splash of colour, isn't it?' During a hot spell, Mrs Gray waters the begonias three times a day. 'People are always saying to me, "How do you get such big begonias?". Well, it's just a question of masses to drink and some good manure. Never let them go dry.' There is a winter jasmine either side of the front door and cineraria maritima beside the steps and, apart from the honeysuckle and cotoneaster which the birds planted, Mrs Gray has planted 'Mrs Cholmondely' clematis, euonymus, hydrangea, pyracantha, bay, fuchsia, phlox and 'Iceberg' roses. 'Despite all those,' says Mrs Gray, 'I still manage to squeeze in a few of my favourite annuals like cornflower and Baby Blue Eyes.'

Clanfield, Oxfordshire. Mr Goddard's summer bedding is made up of lobelia and alyssum edging the pathway, then salvias, petunias and finally snap-dragons.

Hinton-on-the-Green, Worcestershire. This tiny garden photographed in early June will fill out to become a thick carpet of colour by August.

MRS Alexander was born here nearly sixty years ago and used to help her father in the garden as a child. When he died in 1941, and her husband was away in the navy, she began looking after it herself and has done so ever since. Mr Alexander, who is now retired, helps with the heavy digging, fencing and the meticulous planning of vegetable rotation. The present front garden layout was done in 1963. Mrs Alexander planned it all from the upstairs bedroom window, though she had the passers-by in mind. 'It does encourage you so when people stop to look,' she says. The summer bedding is usually made of lobelias, salvias, nemesias, ageratum, dahlias, asters, marigolds and pansies. Living on very sandy soil,

Mrs Alexander says that trying to keep up a lawn is more trouble than flowers and vegetables, so she's given up the idea and has gravel paths between the beds. Although she saves all her own seed, she still spends about £10 a year on the garden in the form of lime, peat, dried blood and fresh seed. 'If you go on using the same seed year after year you get back to the original colour of the plant which might not always be what you want.' She is lucky enough to have a brewery nearby which uses dray horses and can get a regular supply of free manure. Mrs Alexander insists that she is not an expert: 'It's all done by trial and error,' she says. 'You learn as you go along.'

Leominster, Herefordshire. Gladioli are backed by standard roses, some of which are twenty years old, including 'Peace', 'Daily Sketch' and 'Superstar'.

Malton, Yorkshire. A classic spring garden of today. The tulips will be replaced by summer bedding at the end of May.

MR and Mrs Colquohoun moved from Sunderland to Stickney three years ago. When they first found their bungalow it was only half finished and stood marooned in a rough field. Apart from completing the building work, they also laid out the garden from scratch.

Mr Colquohoun believes that a garden should be a very happy place and that you should be aware of the atmosphere: 'I think the plants, the flowers and vegetables share our joy. If we are enjoying it and we're happy with them, then they're happy with us.' Mr Colquohoun has been an engineer all his life and explains that his garden is probably a result of his tidy mind. 'There are few curves in engineering,' he says, 'the majority of them are straight lines measured carefully and you have a sense of proportion and you like to carry out that training, I think, in all walks of life.' He likes to have everything square and right and brings on at least five thousand bedding plants each year, which go to make up his spectacular display.

'Orderliness in the home I think is extended into the garden, and the majority of people enjoy it. There are the odd ones who say they don't like that sort of thing, they like everything in a turmoil and an uproar. I'm afraid we don't belong to that school.'

Honington, Warwickshire. The in-between stage during early June when alyssum, lobelias, marigolds, petunias and dahlias have yet to reach their peak.

ABOVE
Heddington, Wiltshire. For spring colour it is hard to beat the rich glow of wallflowers—particularly against red brick.

RIGHT
Dagenham, Essex. This garden has won numerous prizes. Mr Miller is unwilling to divulge his special formula for the lawn.

Pickering, Yorkshire. Yellow 'Georgette' and red 'Halcro' tulips make a formidable splash in a suburb of Pickering.

Newent, Gloucestershire. Standard hybrid tea roses line the drive, set in beds of red, white and blue geraniums, alyssum and lobelias.

Informal Gardens

Little Coxwell, Berkshire.
'I talk to my flowers and fuss them a lot,' says Mrs Minterne, who
comes from a farming family. Marigolds are her favourites.

MR Parker has lived in 'Lansdowne' on and off since 1908, when his father built the house on the main A44. Although in his seventies, Mr Parker still grows asparagus by Royal Appointment. He has won the championships at the local flower show three times. 'I just do the front garden as I think best,' says Mr Parker, 'though I have an unusual amount of pyrethemums because they're my favourite. My wife thinks a wonderful lot of pelargoniums—we put some in the front this summer and we like begonias and things like that. I think the frost got the white and yellow ones this year.' Mr Parker comes from a family of ten.

'My father was the Broadway postman and my brother is the gardener up at the big house; they've all been in gardening in their time my family—some in landscaping and some in market gardening.' Mrs Parker helps with weeding and fruit picking, but it's Mr Parker who is the mainstay of the garden. 'I spend all my time in the garden, I suppose, except when I go and look after an old lady's garden up the road. I think good manure is the secret of healthy plants. I don't think my garden's much better than anyone else's but there were these people up from Kent last week who said what a lovely show it was, and that made my day.'

Windley, Derbyshire. The garden was a jungle when Mr and Mrs Bliss first came. 'Bliss,' advised a neighbour, 'I should get an elephant and shoot tigers through it.'

Fairford, Gloucestershire. Mrs Coomer's pathside bed is cut in waves on the lawn side and includes aquilegias, pyrethrums, eschscholzias, cornflowers and flax.

East Tytherton, Wiltshire. Mrs Penny grows an informal mixture of lupins, delphiniums, anchusa, sweet williams, cranesbill, pink candytuft and French marigolds.

Cholmondely, Cheshire. 'If you want a good show,' says Mr Williams, 'you must feed liquid manure.' He chooses 'New Dawn' roses for their long blooming period.

MR Link has lived in the village of Edensor for most of his forty-five years. His father was the head gardener at Chatsworth for forty years and his uncle is also a keen gardener. 'I can't go wrong really,' says Mr Link, 'because my family all live nearby and the topic of gardening never stops buzzing round the village. People are always talking about when they put their beans in or when they lift their potatoes. I grow ornamental cabbages in the flower beds which causes quite a stir and some people think they are made of rice paper.'

Mr Link's wife works as a nurse and takes a keen interest in the garden. 'I love to see the garden nice. Though my husband is the boss I am allowed to do the boring things like mowing and edging, and of course the stone troughs are my department. I usually fill them with those tiny violas although one year I filled them with mesembryanthemums and that looked lovely. I'd be lost without a garden.'

Mr Link is not obsessed with gardening, he'd just as soon go and play a game of golf as weed the garden. Nonetheless his display is one of the best for miles around and his white delphiniums which he grows from seed are the talk of the village. 'Sometimes gardening is a drudge,' he says, 'but you get that satisfied feeling when you've done it, and you can look out of your sitting-room window and say "that looks nice".'

LEFT
Holford, Herefordshire. Rather like the house, lupins and red hot pokers rise surprisingly from behind a privet hedge, to be followed on by lilies.

RIGHT
Westmancote, Worcestershire. Mr Walls's father built the house in 1926 and the Michaelmas daisies have spread along the path for as long as Mr Walls can remember.

BELOW
Wroughton, Wiltshire. Gertrude Jekyll was very fond of crimson hollyhocks. They tend to suffer from rust, but do well in smoke-polluted areas.

Castleton, Derbyshire. When Mrs
Barnes tamed a corner of the church yard
which adjoins her house, the vicar said:
'I've seen a miracle grow before my eyes.

Colwall Green, Worcestershire. One of
the secrets of Miss Turner's and Miss
Mitchell's important shrub garden is the
use of an inordinate amount of peat.

MR Dyer has lived here all his life, as his parents and grand-parents did before him. Although the house has been re-built, the garden layout has remained basically the same. Mr Dyer left school at thirteen and became a farm worker for ten shillings a week with a shilling a year rise. Later he started working as a gardener at Overbury Court where he remained until his retirement. He used to go in for flower shows a lot then and once he won a hundred pints of free beer in the local pub as a prize for his vegetables. 'I learnt most of what I know about gardening from my mother and father, but then you gain experience going along through life.' Now Mr Dyer is retired nothing will keep him away from his own garden. 'He wants his bed out there some nights,' says Mrs Dyer. There are a lot of tame birds about the place, a thrush being the most daring of all: 'He sits on my spade happy as anything.' Mr Dyer believes in overcrowding his garden: 'You can't get a good continuation of things otherwise. There's always something blooming here and if anything seeds itself, it usually stays. That laburnum tree was seeded by a bird seventy years ago and look at it now. There are some roses I'd never be without—"Caroline Testout", "Queen Elizabeth", "Masquerade", "Super Star"—but the best is "Fragrant Cloud", you've got a job to beat that.'

Fladbury, Worcestershire. The sight of these two gardens causes most passing motorists to slow down—the Cancer relief collection box at the gate collects a tidy sum.

Bath, Somerset. Imagine this Victorian window without the kerria and cotoneastor beneath it and the tumbling sea of perenial candytuft before it.

Ornamental Gardens

Clacton-on-Sea, Essex.
The creator of this shell garden took only three years to build it, when in his eighties. All the shells are from the local beach.

SADLY Mr William Talbot died earlier this year but he will be remembered forever as the creator of one of the finest front gardens in the land. In a tiny plot in front of his council house he built no less than thirteen cathedrals and churches. Dwarf conifers dotted about between give scale to the architecture, lights glint through the stained glass windows and a sound system wafts church music over the pavement.

Mr Talbot was a coal miner all his life and first went down the local pits at thirteen. He retired eleven years ago and it was then that he first began his building. 'One day some builders over t'other side had half a bucket of cement left and they come to me and they said: "Bill, could you do anything with this?"

So I thought to myself, here goes, I'll do a little model of Measham church.' As he gained experience, each church got better although he tried the crooked tower of Chesterfield twelve times before it finally came right. The cement kept bulging out, but he eventually built it up by putting a little piece on every day, letting it dry, and putting a little more on the next day until he got to the top. Out of the thirteen, he likes Lincoln and York Minster best. Apart from Cologne and Lichfield cathedrals there is also Coventry which Mr Talbot always dreamed of recreating. 'I can just fancy myself standing there and saying to myself, Bill, you've got to do this, and I didn't settle till I'd done it.'

BELOW AND RIGHT
Paddington, London. Mr Bushnell runs a car hire business. He has used old dustbins, lavatory pans and inverted tin helmets to hold his plants.

ABOVE
Colney Park, Norfolk. Mrs Wink first got the idea to make papier mâché animals for her garden when she visited a pleasure park in the Isle of Wight.

The GARDENERS PRAYER
Great God of little things...
Look upon our Labours....
Make our little Gardens....
A little better than our Neighbours.

MR Johnson, who has just retired from being the lock-keeper on the canal, lives here with his daughter and son-in-law. There was nothing fancy about the garden when they first came. Mr Johnson was brought up by his grandmother at Blakeley near Manchester where they had a largish garden and he picked up gardening at an early age. His son-in-law does all the painting on the poles and an old gentleman who lives nearby does the traditional barge painting on the house. 'I'm quite surprised that people like our garden,' says Mr Johnson. 'The birds don't seem to appreciate it—we've had all those bird boxes up for four years now and we've never had a bird near them! That dog came off a rubbish tip and the wheels are from an old corn drill.' Mr Johnson planted the 'Queen Elizabeth' roses in memory of his late wife because they were her favourite. 'Some of the other roses must be a hundred years old,' he says, 'the old canal inspector's father put in most of them before 1900.' Mr Johnson is seventy-six. 'They tell me I'm getting old, but I keep myself fit in the garden. I can't understand people who don't keep up a garden, perhaps they're too fond of the good life.'

MR Sweet built 'Dunromin' in 1949 and started the garden from scratch. He comes from a Somerset farming family. 'Ever since I was a boy, growing things has been a natural desire,' he says. 'The cypresses were planted in 1952, and the enormous laburnum arch over the front gates started from a stray seed the birds dropped twelve years ago. Although Mr Sweet's favourite shrubs are magnolias and rhododendrons, he just can't make them grow in his chalky soil. 'I like to give a bit of colour to other people,' he says, 'that's why I plant up the verge.' Mr Sweet swaps plants with friends and relations in Somerset and always tries to get to the Chelsea Flower Show each year to get new ideas. 'I like things to be as neat and tidy as possible— that's why I don't like things like forget-me-nots because they take over if you're not careful, and my doctor says I mustn't do too much bending down.' Mr Sweet makes all his own plaster ornaments which sit along the front wall and he also grows his own pipe tobacco. 'If you want a good garden,' he says, 'you have to use your common sense and plant things properly in the first place.'

LEFT
Bournemouth, Dorset. This now famous garden on the sea front took twenty-five years to create and contains mementoes from all over the world. Its creator was in the navy.

BELOW
Salisbury, Wiltshire. Mr Hartley had over three hundred ornaments in his garden before vandals stole a lot of them. He paints the tips of his daffodils.

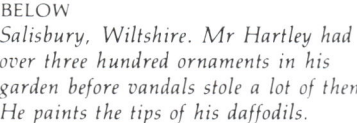

LEFT
Lambourne, Berkshire. The owner of this garden is a retired blacksmith and has a lighthouse on a small island in the brook which runs before his door.

Cottage
Gardens

Shawbury, Shropshire.
The Misses Foulkes have lived here since 1939 and say, 'We have Mr
Woolworth to thank for a lot of our roses!'

WHEN Mrs Coleman first came to Thatch Cottage fifty-five years ago: 'It was terrible,' she says. 'Great high hedges everywhere so you couldn't see out of the windows and stacks of rubbish.' Although the garden looks spectacular enough in summer, Mrs Coleman insists that in spring it's even better: 'It's glorious then,' she says, 'with wallflowers and bulbs, and hyacinths poking through cushions of pink and blue forget-me-nots, and from the road it looks ever so effective.' She uses bonemeal a lot because it's slow acting. She doesn't talk or sing to the flowers but she empties her tea pot on to the clematis. An old gentleman told her that if you cut the roses back when they've bloomed to about the third leaf from the flower, you get another crop of roses the same year. She never bothers to remember the proper names of plants but simply calls them by the names of people who gave them to her—Mrs Pratt and Mrs Coombe and so on.

Mrs Coleman gardens because she enjoys it. 'They say "Nearer God's Heart in a Garden", and, although I'm not religious, if I'm ever troubled I can go out in the garden and forget everything. I've met lovely people through my garden, and only because of the garden. There's an old master from Eton College who comes every year, he's ninety-four now and he says to me: "You don't mind how long I sit in your garden do you? It's so peaceful and beautiful." You certainly get rewarded for what you've done.'

Hopton Heath, Shropshire. A cottage garden can withstand neglect and even be enhanced by an unkempt quality.

BELOW AND RIGHT
Little Coxwell, Berkshire. If you ask an old timer what flower he most remembers as a child it is either the everlasting pea by the door, or the hollyhocks against the wall.

MRS Meredith is always up by 6 a.m. 'You've got to keep at it to get it done,' she says about her garden. 'Lorry drivers get a good view of it from the main road and quite often they bring their wives back with them the following week and stop to have a look.' Despite the fact that Mrs Meredith has spinal trouble she still works in the garden almost all the time. 'I just happen to love dabbling in the earth.' She likes things to seed themselves all over the place, 'because then you have less weeds. They say round here that I've got green fingers—well I'm not one of your Percy Thrower type gardeners, I don't go by the book—I just plant a thing and say "live or die". There was that tree peony over there which never flowered for three years and I said to it, "you've got one more chance", and I moved it and this year it's full of flowers.'

The only thing in the garden which Mrs Meredith doesn't much like are the red hot pokers which the lady over the road gave her. 'She died not long ago, and I haven't the heart to dig them up.' A friend from Dymock gave her the white irises which have spread like wild fire and her next door neighbour, Burt Wood, gave her an unidentified yellow rose which she calls 'Burt Wood'. 'People say to me: "Mrs M, you haven't got a 'Superstar rose'"—well, I can't see anything in them myself—give me my "Prima Ballerina" or my "Shot Silk" any day.'

MR Newnham was brought up in Chastleton and came to this cottage in 1952. 'It was wild then,' he says, 'and we grew vegetables at first. After a bit we started adding flowers, and now it's like this. It's a lot of work but you don't see many gardens like this, do you? It's a crazy garden but we love it—we spend hours out here and sometimes we forget to wash up the breakfast things till dinner time.' Mr and Mrs Newnham are both seventy-four and their favourite flowers are lily-of-the-valley. Mr Newnham buds most of his own roses onto briars which he gets from the hedgerows in autumn. The euonymus was here long before Mr Newnham. 'The cottage used to belong to the school teacher and she said it was there long before her time. So was the moss rose and the 'Gloire de Dijon' rose, which means they must be a hundred years old at least. The hollyhocks grow higher than the thatch when they're in full flight— they must have been here twenty-five years —in their early days they were double, but now they've gone single.' Mrs Newnham brings on a lot of rock rose cuttings by placing a stone over a stem so that it roots itself, and then she waters the stone so as not to flood the baby roots. She then cuts the old stem away when the roots are established. Mr Newnham finds the odd fossils up at the nearby Roman Rissington Camp, and places them about the garden. 'We love our garden,' he says, 'it's not a labour in vain.'

Broadstone, Shropshire. Pinks, hydrangeas, snapdragons, geraniums, honeysuckle and 'New Dawn' roses by the doorway and delphiniums, valerian and lysimachia in the foreground.

Ashbury, Berkshire. Hollyhocks thriving in chalky soil against a cottage at the foot of the Berkshire downs.

MR Martin was brought up in 'O So Cosy' and came back to live here again with his wife in 1918. They are both in their seventies and Mrs Martin helps in the garden sometimes but it's mainly Mr Martin's affair. 'I don't give in easy,' he says. 'Mustn't sit about, just keep at it.' The garden has the same lay out as it did in 1918. 'It was nearly all veg then, 'course you had to have all veg then, they were hard times. I like those godetias in the front. I don't know how long they've been there, they seed themselves every year so I just let them stop there. Some of the roses are my dad's. The white one over there was struck by my dad from a cutting he brought back from Bognor Regis in 1910.' Mrs Martin likes hydrangeas and pelargoniums the best. In the small bed surrounded by the godetias Mr Martin does a different bedding-out arrangement each year. 'In Jubilee Year, we had red and white geraniums in there and they were blooming away, then what do you think happened? Out of nowhere comes this blue iris right in the middle. We couldn't believe it—red white and blue for Jubilee year. Oh yes, I'm one of the old sort—I like old-fashioned flowers: hollyhocks and fuchsias in pots. They took pride in their gardens years ago, and I'm doing the best I can now.'

(Since this interview was written, the garden has disappeared and the house has been boarded up)

Elmley Castle, Worcestershire. A small stream banked by wild irises, ferns and sedges runs between this cottage and the pavement.

Wick Hill, Wiltshire. 'If a lawn is tidy and mown,' says Miss Bridget Parke, 'then everything else looks slightly better.'

Vegetable Gardens

Malton, Yorkshire.
A large vegetable garden in early spring. About seventy per cent of English gardens have vegetable plots but only thirty-four per cent have fruit.

MRS Ball has lived here for nearly forty years, and since her husband died a few years ago, her son who lives just up the village street has been seeing to her vegetables for her. 'You need your veg if you live in the country,' says Mrs Ball, and she has certainly never dreamt of converting any of the garden into lawn like the people who have moved in nearby. 'They've grassed in the whole front plot,' she says, 'and I think that's a real waste—what's the point of having a garden if you don't grow your own vegetables?' Mrs Ball has flowers around her door and directly in front of the house and a small bed at the end of the garden under the wall which lines the pavement. The flowers are her responsibility and she grows madonna lilies, Michaelmas daisies, peonies, delphiniums, pyrethrums and a variety of spring bulbs. Her son spends a few hours a week on the vegetables which he grows from seed and feeds regularly with manure from the local farm. There is an apple and a plum tree among the neat rows, and, although the vegetables do not grow so well in their shade, the fruit they produce for making jams and jellies certainly makes them worth keeping. 'There's nothing my son doesn't grow,' says Mrs Ball, 'except runner beans which we don't like one bit. But peas, now that's a different matter— there's nothing in the world to touch the taste of fresh garden peas.'

'PEOPLE say to me, "You'll live till you're a hundred and fifty—it's so peaceful in your garden."' Mr Saunders has been here fifty-five of his seventy-odd years already.

He started work as a gardener at nearby Sherbourne Park in 1912, along with seventeen other gardeners and still pops down there once a week to see how things are getting on. 'Gardening's a disease,' says Mr Saunders. 'I could never stop it. In 1973 I grew a marrow weighing 34½ lbs, and I had my photograph in the *People* newspaper. I've won prizes with honey too, I've kept bees since I was ten years old. The fruit is that much better with bees, you know.' Mrs Saunders helps in the garden, 'But she'd rather scrub a room than weed a bed,' says her husband. Mr Saunders believes in mix-ing vegetables with flowers: 'The veg are good to eat and the flowers are good to smell. If you can please both parts of the body, you're well away, aren't you? I have most of the flowers going down the path so it's nice for people walking in, and some more along the house so we can smell them from the windows. I like old-fashioned things the best—tiger lilies for looks and honeysuckle, pinks and night-scented stocks for smell. There's always something out— Christmas roses, lent lilies, and the cabbages don't look bad.' The magnolia soulangeana was there before Mr Saunders—he feeds it with Epsom Salts. His favourite rose is 'Zepherin', which has no thorns. 'Every garden should have one,' he says.

LEFT
East Tytherton, Wiltshire. Mr Baker grows a profusion of flowers next to his garden path with vegetables either side.

ABOVE
Old Arlesford, Hampshire. Mr Mellish has devoted the whole of his large front garden to vegetables, though roses and foxgloves grow next to the house.

LEFT
South Creek, Norfolk. They say the cabbage family, strawberries and beans actively dislike being planted next to onions. Carrots, on the other hand, are happy close by.

Topiary

Lawshall, Suffolk.
Mr Boast started his topiary menagerie about eight years ago. Being a
shepherd by trade, he uses sheep shears to trim it.

'I ALWAYS wanted to be an artist and go to art school but I couldn't, so now topiary is my art. When I first started I wanted to do things that had never been done before in topiary—I've obviously got the gift. When I began the horse and jockey, my wife said I'd gone off my rocker and it couldn't be done. I did it, though, and there it was for everyone to see. The eagle was very difficult to do, but I don't use wire to help me, I leave wire well alone. I'd challenge any professional on that.' The topiary is mostly made up of privet which Mr Rivers plaits in order to shape it to what he wants. On the basket already growing against the house, he intends to grow a cat, but his most ambitious scheme of all is to be a military crest on a yew tree which is not yet big enough to shape. 'I've always had it in me, that's obvious,' says Mr Rivers. 'We get so many people slowing down in their cars to take a look, that I've almost stopped noticing them. What I can't understand is why these big stately homes don't have more topiary work to bring the crowds in. All you see is balls on top of squares and there's no point to them.' Mr Rivers' advice for success is to have a first class pair of secateurs, 'as sharp as a razor, or you bruise the stems—and don't clip in the sun or you'll get brown leaves. I said I'd make my name famous—and I will!'

Ugley, Suffolk. A traditional cottage topiary bird of yew. Myriad cottage gardens sported one from the eighteenth century onwards.

Long Hanborough, Oxfordshire. Mr Leach created this replica of the V and W Class Destroyer (H.M.S. Verity) on which he served as a leading torpedo operator.

THERE wasn't much of a garden here thirty-eight years ago—just one golden privet bush which Mrs Stokes was about to pull out and throw away, when she thought: 'No, I'll get the dubbers and cut into it.' Gradually the chair evolved. 'It just came to me,' she says. 'I didn't get the idea from anywhere except in my own head.' Mrs Stokes thought it looked so nice that she then grew two more armchairs. 'I'm going to make a peacock one day,' she says. Mr and Mrs Stokes work together as a team. They are both in their seventies. 'We help one another inside and outside the house,' says Mrs Stokes. 'What he can't do, I do and vice versa.' Mr Stokes' grandfather was a gardener at nearby Cholmondely Castle, so the art runs in the family. There are two tame sparrows in the garden who eat out of Mr Stokes' hand. He calls them 'Joey' and 'Cocky'. 'I like to be in the garden every possible moment,' says Mr Stokes. 'Last year our dahlias were gigantic, but they haven't done so well this year.' Apart from her work in the garden Mrs Stokes also paints the outside of the cottage once a year. 'We won the prize for the best kept garden last year. We get no end of folks coming to have a look—some from Manchester and even Blackpool!'

MR Gregg's topiary is mostly made of privet which he grew from slips nearly forty years ago. He trained the stems round bits of wire to get the shapes. 'I didn't copy the idea from anywhere,' he says, 'it just came to me.' Mr Gregg's least favourite job is clipping the privet once a fortnight in the growing season. He must have clipped it nearly 5,000 times. Enclosed by the topiary in the spring are a mass of daffodils, tulips, polyanthus, auriculas, grape hyacinths and wallflowers. Mr Gregg carries out a rigorous routine with his bulbs every year. He digs them up in May, heels them in in the back garden until September when he lifts them, dries them out and plants them again in October. In the summer he beds out begonias, snapdragons, dahlias and marguerites. He developed an interest in gardening when he was at school in Cardiff and he also got inspired by the gardens at Blenheim which are just up the road from Kidlington. 'I wouldn't say I was a proper gardener—I don't even know the names of most of the plants—I just do it to make the place nice and tidy.'

Horringer, Suffolk. For large topiary work, yew is undoubtedly the best medium, and, once shape is established, need only be clipped once a year.

Wickhambrook, Suffolk. These birds are of red may. 'Mine is a pheasant,' says Mr Coe, 'and I should think Mr Bannister's is a chicken, wouldn't you?'

Banks and Verges

Broadstone, Shropshire.
This bank, visible only from the village street, includes bergenias, lamb's
ears, rock roses, cranesbill, Californian poppies and 'Masquerade' roses.

WHEN Mrs Mould, a school meals supervisor, retired recently she said to herself: 'I must have enough to do.' So she dug up the verge ('the council didn't seem to mind') and planted it up with bits from her garden and various plants which friends gave her. 'It cost me nothing at all,' says Mrs Mould, 'except a bit of time.' She likes to get out as much as she can and look at famous gardens round about. 'The trouble is, when I get back here I get so depressed, I mean compared to any of those, mine is nothing.' Mrs Mould's cottage has been in the family for a hundred-and-fifty years. When her ninety-one-year-old aunty came to visit her the other day, she remembered the japonica by the front door being there when she was a child. 'I love the feeling that I'm keeping things going, and I suppose through nostalgia I go on planting all the old-fashioned things like Lady's Needlework and Bunny's Ears. I spend an awful lot of time in the garden, but I take it quite gently. People passing say to me: "Isn't your garden nice," and that's the sort of thing that makes it all worthwhile.'

Hatford, Berkshire. Hollyhocks have been known to grow to a height of eighteen to twenty feet. Apparently they thrive on beer.

Rickinghall, Suffolk. A generous spring display, including the sturdy 'Tambour Maitre' tulip, outside a privet hedge which borders on two roads.

MR Rumming's interest in gardening began when he was at school sixty-odd years ago, and was given his own plot to tend. He grew vegetables as did his parents at their cottage in Highway and the only flower he remembers from his childhood was an everlasting sweet pea round the front door. When Mr Rumming and his wife moved to 'Sandridge' ten years ago, the ground was a mass of stones and thistles. 'You'll never make anything of that,' said his next door neighbour. Today there is not a square inch uncared for. 'I planned all the garden from my own head—I chose aubretia for colour and it also keeps the weeds down.

It's usually pretty trouble-free except for a couple of years ago when the mice played havoc with it.' Mr Rumming saves all his own seed and brings on all his own, and his next door neighbour's, bedding plants in the latter's greenhouse. He took 170 cuttings of geraniums and pelargoniums last year, and only lost a dozen. He spends £2 a year on bulbs and about £5 on peat and lawn fertilizer. He always watches 'Gardener's World' with his wife and believes the secret of gardening is hard work and plenty of farm yard manure. 'People quite often stop in front of our garden and just look—we really enjoy that!'

Hinton-on-the-Green, Worcestershire. Four plants of 'Paul's Scarlet Climber' rose have taken only three years to cover this fence.

Brimscombe, Gloucestershire. The local council did not accept Mr and Mrs Williams's offer to continue their flowering bank on virgin bank adjoining theirs.

Great Bircham, Norfolk.
Alternate 'Preludium' and 'Red Giant' tulips, mixed with polyanthus
and aubretia, outside the garden gate.